MACHINES CLOSE-UP

RESCUE VEHICLES

Daniel Gilpin and Alex Pang

This edition published in 2013 by Wayland

Wayland
Hachette Children's Books
338 Euston Road
London NW1 3BH

Wayland Australia
Level 17/207 Kent Street
Sydney, NSW 2000

Produced by

David West  Children's Books
7 Princeton Court
55 Felsham Road
London SW15 1AZ

Designer: Gary Jeffrey
Illustrator: Alex Pang
Editor: Katharine Pethick
Consultant: Steve Parker

A CIP catalogue record for this book is available
from the British Library.

ISBN: 9780750280266

2 4 6 8 10 9 7 5 3 1

Printed in China

Wayland is a division of
Hachette Children's Books,
an Hachette UK company.
www.hachette.co.uk

PHOTO CREDITS :
Abbreviations: t-top, m-middle, b-bottom, r-right,
l-left, c-centre.
4b, US Army; 6l, skuds; 6b, Rozalyn Dorsay;
7tr, Library of Congress; 7ml, Wyrdlight; 7bl,
gsloan; 7br, dave_7; 30t, Dtom; 8t, lifeboat rnli;
8b, Mariners Weather Log; 9t, Bmpower; 30m,
Bell Helicopter; 30b, carbon motors corp;

CONTENTS

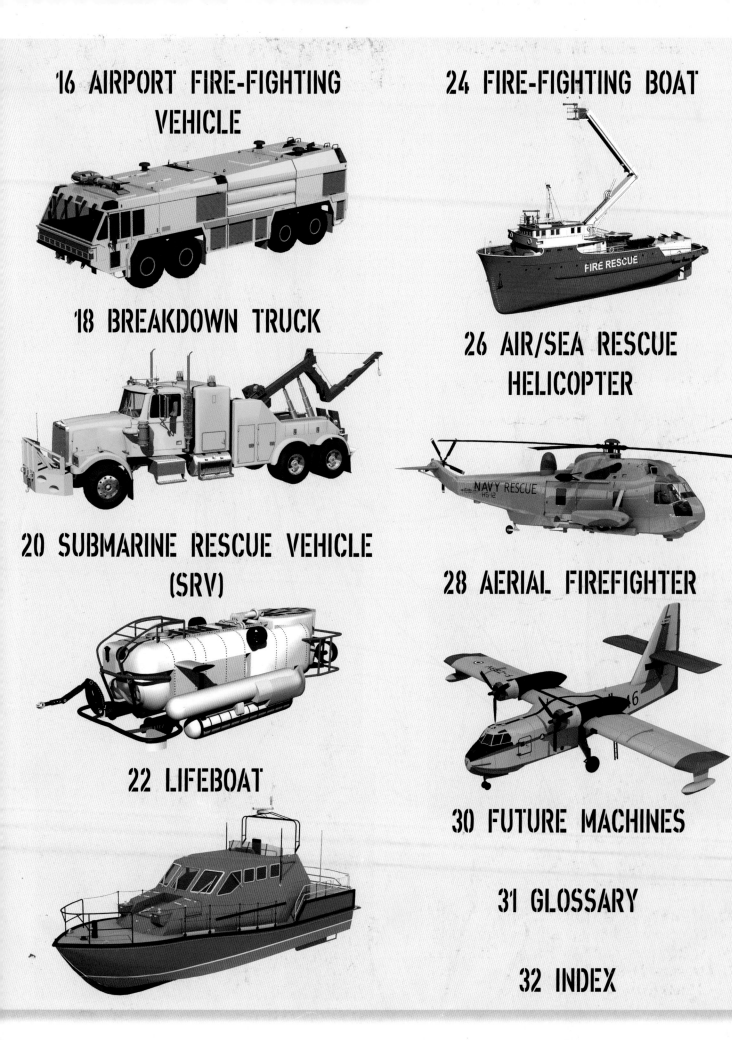

INTRODUCTION

Rescue vehicles are a part of modern life, their sirens a familiar sound in our towns and cities. Many of us take them for granted and forget the important role they play. The reality is that without them the world would be a much more dangerous place to live in.

MACHINES TO THE RESCUE
Motorised vehicles and their operators are a vital part of most emergency services, working on land, air and sea to protect property and save people's lives.

HOW THIS BOOK WORKS

MAIN TEXT

The introduction text explains the history of the vehicle and outlines its primary role. Information, such as which services use the vehicle, is also covered here.

MAIN CUTAWAY

This exploded illustration shows the internal structure of the vehicle and gives information on the positions of its various working parts.

EQUIPMENT

Smaller illustrations look in detail at the specialised equipment carried by the vehicle and used by the people who operate it, to carry out different roles.

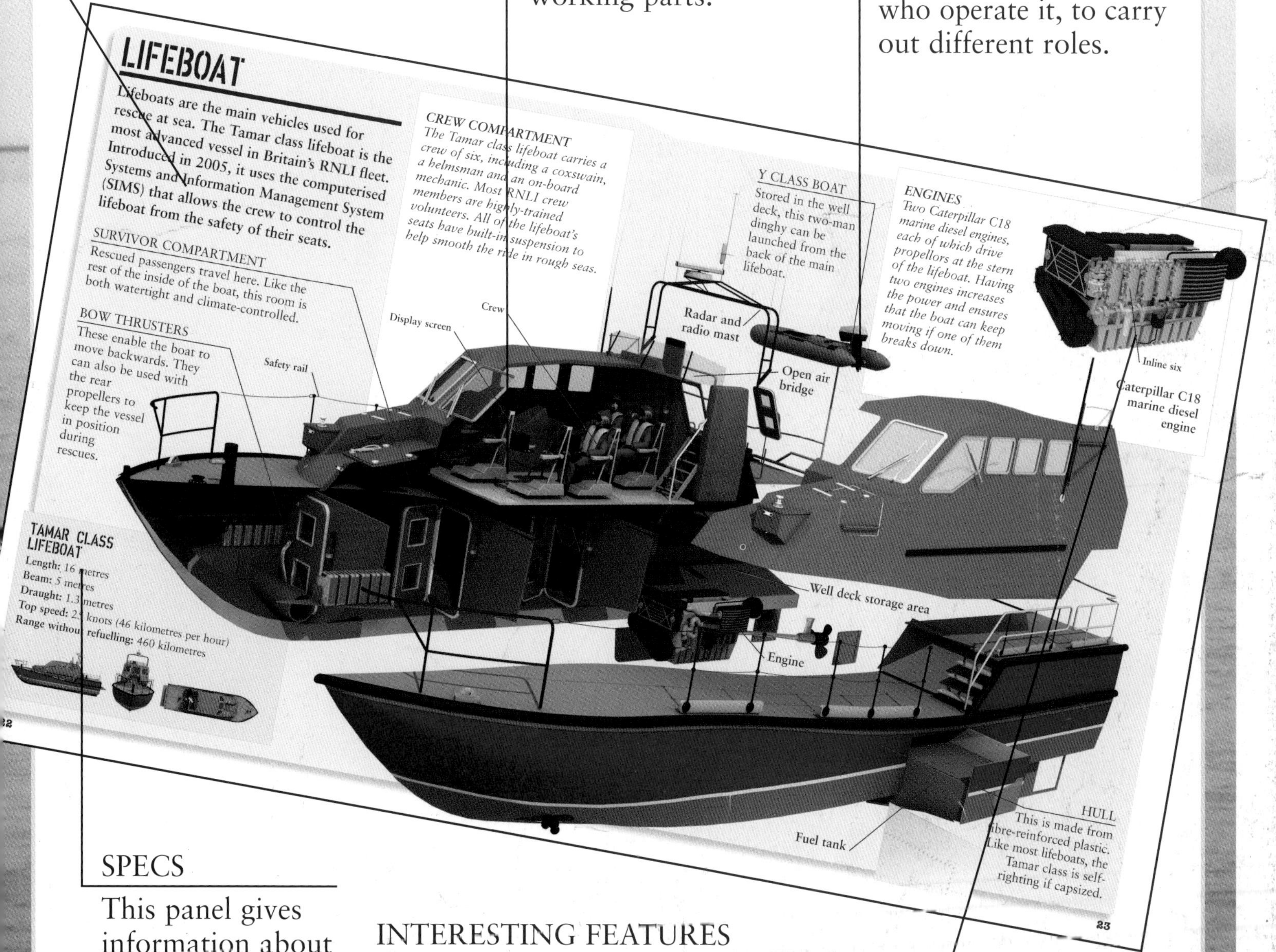

LIFEBOAT

Lifeboats are the main vehicles used for rescue at sea. The Tamar class lifeboat is the most advanced vessel in Britain's RNLI fleet. Introduced in 2005, it uses the computerised Systems and Information Management System (SIMS) that allows the crew to control the lifeboat from the safety of their seats.

SURVIVOR COMPARTMENT
Rescued passengers travel here. Like the rest of the inside of the boat, this room is both watertight and climate-controlled.

BOW THRUSTERS
These enable the boat to move backwards. They can also be used with the rear propellers to keep the vessel in position during rescues.

CREW COMPARTMENT
The Tamar class lifeboat carries a crew of six, including a coxswain, a helmsman and an on-board mechanic. Most RNLI crew members are highly-trained volunteers. All of the lifeboat's seats have built-in suspension to help smooth the ride in rough seas.

Y CLASS BOAT
Stored in the well deck, this two-man dinghy can be launched from the back of the main lifeboat.

ENGINES
Two Caterpillar C18 marine diesel engines, each of which drive propellors at the stern of the lifeboat. Having two engines increases the power and ensures that the boat can keep moving if one of them breaks down.

Inline six

Caterpillar C18 marine diesel engine

Crew

Display screen

Safety rail

Radar and radio mast

Open air bridge

Well deck storage area

Engine

Fuel tank

HULL
This is made from fibre-reinforced plastic. Like most lifeboats, the Tamar class is self-righting if capsized.

TAMAR CLASS LIFEBOAT
Length: 16 metres
Beam: 5 metres
Draught: 1.3 metres
Top speed: 25 knots (46 kilometres per hour)
Range without refuelling: 460 kilometres

SPECS

This panel gives information about the vehicle's speed, dimensions and operational range.

INTERESTING FEATURES

This box contains a detailed illustration of the engine or another design feature that makes the vehicle unique. Informative text explains the feature's function.

LAND-BASED RESCUE

The history of the rescue vehicle is a long one. Over the centuries these machines have helped to save countless people. Today they are a regular sight all around the world.

FIRE TENDERS

Fires have always been a problem, particularly in towns and built-up areas. The earliest mechanised fire tenders were developed in the 19th century. The invention of the internal combustion engine saw these horse-drawn units replaced by more modern, self-propelled fire engines.

FIRE HOOKS
In the early 17th century, people used long-handled hooks to pull thatch from roofs to put out fires.

VICTORIAN STEAM PUMPER
The first tenders were horse-drawn, steam-engine-powered pumps.

1950s LADDER TENDER

AIRPORT CRASH TENDER

ARFF VEHICLES

Early Aircraft Rescue and Fire-Fighting vehicles were developed during World War II. This development increased as civil airports offering commercial flights grew in number.

AMBULANCES

Motorised ambulances first appeared in the early 20th century. The concept of the ambulance was well established as horse-drawn municipal ambulances were already in use. Early motorised ambulances were little more than covered trucks, but in time the equipment they carried became more sophisticated.

MILITARY AMBULANCE
Before there were motorised ambulances, people used horses and carts. The first organised ambulance services were military ones.

MODEL T FORD AMBULANCE

1970s CADILLAC AMBULANCE

PATROL CARS

The invention of the patrol car allowed police officers to cover larger areas. By the 1940s, patrol cars were in widespread use in the USA. Soon, other forces began using them in ever greater numbers.

1940s 'BLACK AND WHITE'

1930s FORD WRECKER

BREAKDOWN TRUCKS

Breakdown trucks developed as cars became more common. Not all breakdowns could be fixed at the roadside so specialised vehicles would tow damaged cars away.

AIR AND WATER

The business of saving lives is not confined to land. Boats and aircraft are also used to fight fires and rescue people. These vehicles are often highly specialised.

SEARCH AND RESCUE AT SEA

The history of lifeboats dates back several centuries. The earliest ve... were simple rowing boats... by coastal people to help... trouble off their sho... ...est lifeboat organi... RNLI, founded...

RNLI LIFEBOAT 1936
The men and women of the UK's Royal National Lifeboat Institution have saved many thousands of lives. The organisation is a charity and run largely by volunteers. Since 1980, it has rescued an average of 22 people a day.

US COASTGUARD RESCUE BOAT
In the USA the coastguard combines its main role of monitoring the movement of ships with carrying out rescues at sea.

AIR SEARCH AND RESCUE

Aircraft may also play their part in rescues at sea. Helicopters have been used in this role for more than 50 years. Air search and rescue missions also take place on land, rescuing stranded climbers from cliffs or mountains, for example.

HELICOPTER RESCUE

AERIAL FIRE-FIGHTING

FIRE-FIGHTING FROM AIR AND SEA

Fireboats were designed to tackle blazes on ships, although they can also fight fires in dockland buildings. Aerial fire-fighting machines, such as water bombers, put out fires in forests or in places inaccessible to land-based units.

FIREBOAT
Refurbished vintage vessels like the Edward M Cotter (right), built in 1900, are still used as working fireboats.

SUBMARINE RESCUE

Today there are even vehicles that can rescue people underwater. Submarine rescue vehicles are rare, but so are the accidents that need them. These vehicles and crews often travel long distances to undertake rescue missions.

DEEP SEA RESCUE VEHICLE 2 AVALON

US PATROL CAR

The police are often the first to be called to an accident. Different countries' police forces use different vehicles, but in the USA the Ford Crown Victoria is the most widely used car of all. This model is also sold to the general public, but the police version has several adaptations.

BODYWORK AND CHASSIS

The Ford Crown Victoria has body-on-frame construction. Having a separate body on a rigid frame makes the vehicle easier to repair after minor accidents, because the chassis does not get damaged. Police additions include sirens and emergency lights.

Shotgun

Assault rifle

WEAPONS RACK
Most US police officers carry a shotgun or patrol rifle in the front of the car. So that it is easily accessible but not in the way, it is usually stowed in a weapons rack, either between the seats, or near the dashboard.

Cylinders

Gearbox

Ford V8 petrol engine

Radiator

ENGINE
The Ford Crown Victoria has a 250 horsepower V8 petrol engine, which gives it impressive acceleration when needed. The car is rear-wheel drive and has a four-speed automatic transmission.

Chassis

Laptop computer

INFORMATION SYSTEMS

The modern patrol car has instruments for gathering evidence and keeping in touch with command. The laptop contains GPS software and, together with the printer, allows paperwork to be processed in the field.

Lockable weapons rack

Video camera

TRUNK VAULT

The trunk vault stores evidence or weapons. It keeps these items safe from tampering when the boot of the car is open.

COURTESY
PROFESSIONALISM
RESPECT

5 PCT 2582

BASIC EQUIPMENT

As well as information systems, US police patrol cars carry other electronic equipment, such as radios and digital still cameras.

NYPD

Kevlar-lined front door

FORD CROWN VICTORIA
Length: 5.4 metres
Width: 2.0 metres
Height: 1.4 metres
Wheelbase: 2.9 metres
Top speed: 217 kilometres per hour (limited)

REAR PASSENGER COMPARTMENT

People who have been arrested travel in the rear compartment. The front seats have built-in 'stab plates' to prevent suspects stabbing officers when the car is on the move.

AMBULANCE

An ambulance transports patients to hospital as fast as possible. The latest ambulances carry sophisticated equipment that saves even more lives by offering treatment onboard, before they reach hospital. The Ford E-350 contains all the most commonly needed equipment to keep patients alive during their journey.

Drugs cabinet

Defibrillator unit

Twin rear doors

EMERGENCY EQUIPMENT

Ambulance crews are prepared for all kinds of medical emergencies and the ambulances carry a wide range of equipment. Ambulances usually have a stretcher – a simple bed for carrying patients to and from the vehicle and supporting their bodies inside it. Other more high-tech equipment includes oxygen masks for helping patients with their breathing and defibrillators for restarting the heart.

Stretcher

Defibrillator/monitor

Oxygen system

ONBOARD SYSTEMS

An Advanced Life Support (ALS) ambulance operates like a mobile critical care unit. The onboard system includes a monitor to watch heart rate and other vital signs of life. A ventilator assists with a patient's breathing.

FORD E-350 ADVANCED LIFE SUPPORT AMBULANCE

Length: 6.0 metres
Height: 2.2 metres
Width: 2.0 metres
Wheelbase: 3.5 metres
Maximum load: 1,840 kilograms

Flashing lights

RADIO

Control and the crew exchange information about accidents and casualties by two-way radio.

PARAMEDIC

A highly trained paramedic's priority is to stabilise the patient at the scene, reversing life-threatening conditions that cannot wait for the journey to hospital.

ENGINE

The E-350 has a 6-litre diesel engine. Lights and sirens urge traffic to move out of the way to make the journey as quick as possible.

FIRE ENGINE

Fire engines are the most instantly recognisable rescue vehicles. The international convention is for them to be red and this, combined with their flashing lights and sirens, makes them hard to miss. Most fire engines carry both ladders and hoses, for reaching trapped people as well as putting out fires. Their cabs are usually designed to carry several firefighters, as well as all of their kit.

ENGINE

This needs to be both powerful and reliable – a breakdown during a call-out is the last thing a fire crew needs. This LaFrance fire tender has a 6V Detroit diesel engine.

Sirens

FIREFIGHTERS' EQUIPMENT

Firefighters wear protective clothing to shield them from falling debris and the worst heat of the fire. Breathing apparatus is used when entering burning buildings, as inhaling smoke can be lethal. Other equipment includes hand-held tools such as pike poles and axes, for pulling away burning debris and breaking down doors.

Mask

Fireproof clothing

Breathing apparatus

Breather tank

Regulator

PUMPING EQUIPMENT

In cities, fire engines may use fire hydrants but elsewhere they have to pump water themselves. A built-in pump engine can draw water from an external source, such as a lake or pond, or pump water from a tank on the fire engine.

Pump engine

Hose couplings

Control panel

LAFRANCE FIRE TENDER

Length: 8.2 metres
Width: 2.4 metres
Weight: 14.2 tonnes
Seating capacity: 4
Pumping capacity: 6,820 litres per minute

Extension hoses

LADDERS

A fire crew's main priority is to rescue trapped people and save their lives. Extending ladders raise them to balconies or high windows to get people out of burning buildings.

HOSE REEL

A detachable hose reel means crews can attach hoses to fire hydrants in the street. While the truck is on the move the hose is stored on the reel.

Hose nozzle

AIRPORT FIRE-FIGHTING VEHICLE

Although, statistically, flying is one of the safest ways to travel, accidents do happen. Airports need to be equipped to deal with them. Most large airports have their own fire-fighting vehicles. These are stationed on site, usually in a specially-designed building at the edge of the runway, giving easy access to possible accident sites.

FOAM CANNON
This can be pointed in any direction. Its powerful jet allows the vehicle to remain at a safe distance from the fire.

SNOZZLE
Some airport fire trucks carry a snozzle. This is a long boom arm with a penetrator at the end to pierce the aircraft and spray or inject foam inside. It is operated from the cabin by a joystick and aimed using the high-resolution camera. Floodlights help in smoke or at night.

Foam cannon operator

Injector probe

Hardened steel penetrator

Video camera

Floodlight

CREW CABIN
This houses the driver and the foam cannon operator. The large windscreen and side windows give a wide field of view.

Engine exhaust stacks ———————

FOAM TANKS

Located near the centre of the vehicle, there are two foam tanks, each holding up to 600 litres of foaming agent. Before being sprayed, this is mixed with water which is held in separate tanks.

ENGINES

The Rosenbauer Simba is driven by two Liebherr V8 turbodiesel engines, with a combined output of 1,300 horsepower. The gearbox is fully automatic.

DRIVE TRAIN

This supplies power to all of the Rosenbauer Simba's eight wheels. Having all-wheel drive gives great stability.

Auxiliary equipment

ROSENBAUER SIMBA 8X8 AIRPORT FIRE TRUCK

Length: 12.0 metres
Width: 3.0 metres
Weight: 48 tonnes
Maximum speed: 140 kilometres per hour
Water tank capacity: 11,600 litres

BREAKDOWN TRUCK

Breakdown trucks are among the most common rescue vehicles of all. Their job is to rescue people's broken down vehicles. Most are designed to pull light vehicles, such as cars, but a few are more heavy-duty. The Mack 60 Ton Wrecker is built to tow trucks.

EXHAUST STACKS

These transfer exhaust fumes from the huge engine into the air behind the cab.

CAB

This is where the driver sits. As well as the controls for the tow truck, there is space for a passenger – usually the driver of the broken down truck.

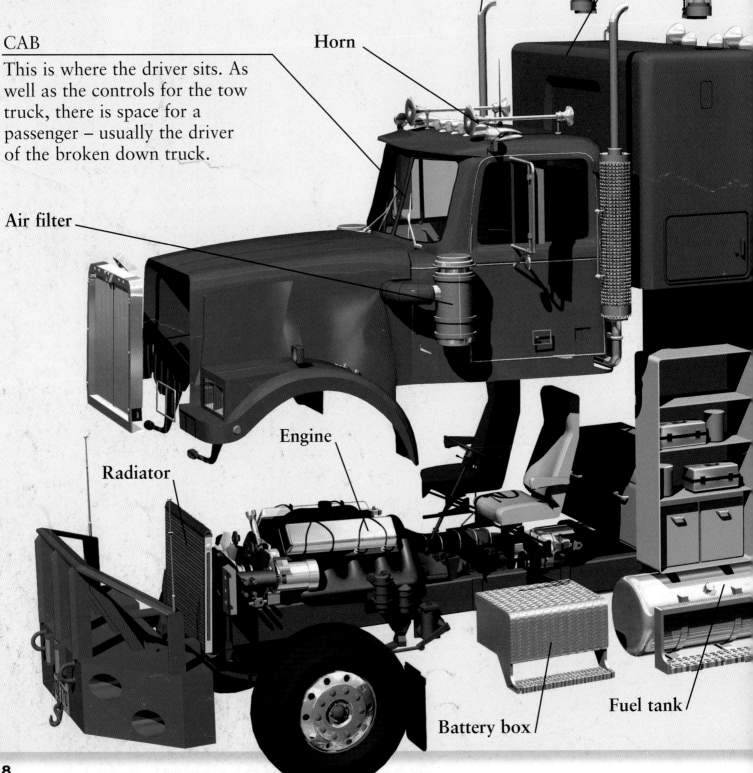

Sleeper cab

Horn

Air filter

Engine

Radiator

Battery box

Fuel tank

BOOM WINCH

This can be used for towing when stowed flat, but it is designed for another job – recovering heavy vehicles that have gone off the road or become stuck where the tow truck cannot reach them.

Hydraulic rams

Tow hook

Articulated winch arm

Brace

MACK 60 TON WRECKER

Length: 8.0 metres
Height: 3.8 metres
Width: 2.6 metres
Wheelbase: 6.2 metres

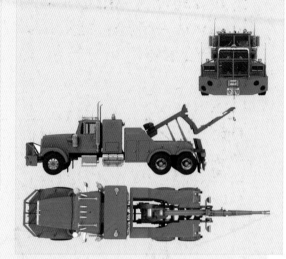

CHASSIS

The Mack 60 Ton Wrecker is a modified Mack Titan and has the same steel chassis, built for strength.

ENGINE AND GEARBOX

A breakdown truck needs a powerful engine to pull its own weight as well as that of another, often heavier vehicle. Like most lorries, the Mack 60 Ton Wrecker has a large number of gears and accelerates very slowly.

9-speed automatic gearbox

Cooling fan

Detroit V8 diesel

SUBMARINE RESCUE VEHICLE (SRV)

There are few places more difficult to perform a rescue than under the sea. Occasionally submarines become entangled and need to be cut loose. If that is not possible then their crews need to be taken back to the surface. This job is undertaken by submarine rescue vehicles like this one.

Protective cage

Top hatch

Thruster

Lateral thruster

SCORPIO ROV

Cutting fishing nets or cables that can become entangled with a submarine is often done with a Remotely Operated Vehicle (ROV) like the Scorpio. Cameras help the operator guide robotic arms to grab and cut.

Manipulator arm

Thruster

Plexiglass dome

Controls

REMOTE ARM

This can shift debris or grab and cut cables. The operator watches its movement through the plexiglass dome.

CREW STATIONS

The NATO SRV has a small crew – the pilot, co-pilot, and rescue chamber operator. During descent, the two pilots sit here.

DOCKING HATCH

The docking hatch has a rubber seal that sits against a submarine's escape hatch. Water is pumped out to create a pressurised seal.

NATO SRV

Length: 10 metres
Weight: 27 tonnes
Maximum operating depth: 610 metres
Maximum submergence time: 96 hours
Top speed: 4 knots (8 kilometres) per hour

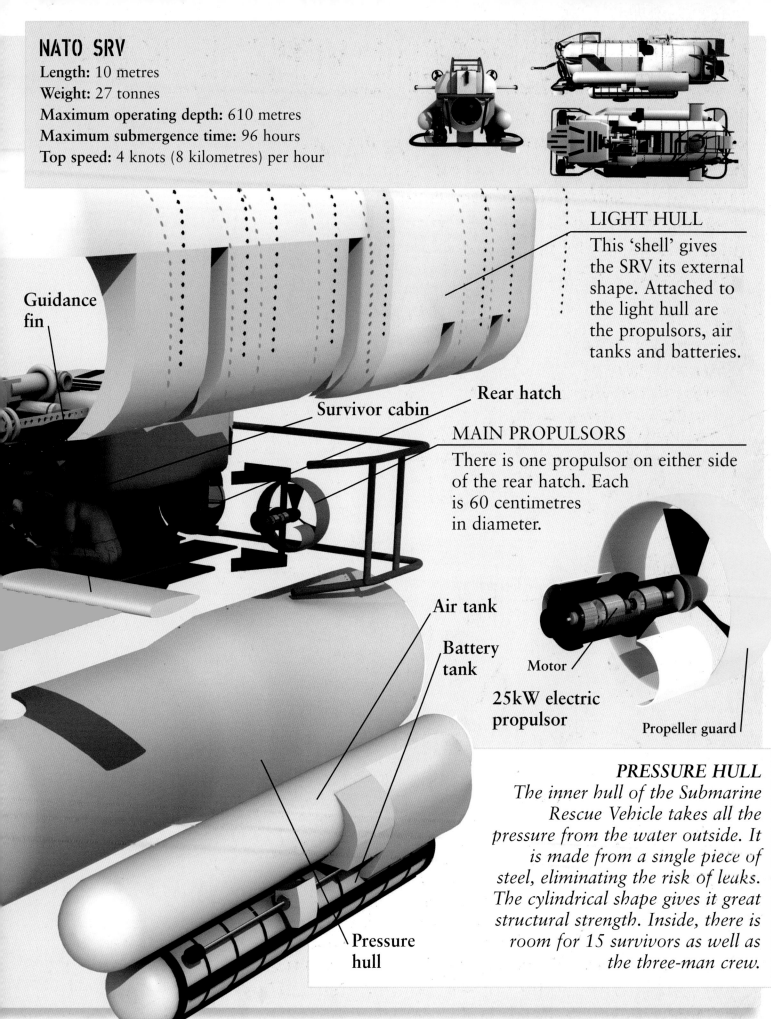

LIGHT HULL

This 'shell' gives the SRV its external shape. Attached to the light hull are the propulsors, air tanks and batteries.

Guidance fin

Survivor cabin

Rear hatch

MAIN PROPULSORS

There is one propulsor on either side of the rear hatch. Each is 60 centimetres in diameter.

Air tank

Battery tank

Motor

25kW electric propulsor

Propeller guard

Pressure hull

PRESSURE HULL

The inner hull of the Submarine Rescue Vehicle takes all the pressure from the water outside. It is made from a single piece of steel, eliminating the risk of leaks. The cylindrical shape gives it great structural strength. Inside, there is room for 15 survivors as well as the three-man crew.

LIFEBOAT

Lifeboats are the main vehicles used for rescue at sea. The Tamar class lifeboat is the most advanced vessel in the UK's RNLI fleet. Introduced in 2005, it uses the computerised Systems and Information Management System (SIMS) that allows the crew to control the lifeboat from the safety of their seats.

SURVIVOR COMPARTMENT

Rescued passengers travel here. Like the rest of the inside of the boat, this room is both watertight and climate-controlled.

BOW THRUSTERS

These enable the boat to move backwards. They can also be used with the rear propellers to keep the vessel in position during rescues.

CREW COMPARTMENT

The Tamar class lifeboat carries a crew of six, including a coxswain, a helmsman and an onboard mechanic. Most RNLI crew members are highly-trained volunteers. All of the lifeboat's seats have built-in suspension to help smooth the ride in rough seas.

Crew

Display screen

Safety rail

TAMAR CLASS LIFEBOAT

Length: 16 metres
Beam: 5 metres
Draught: 1.3 metres
Top speed: 25 knots (46 kilometres per hour)
Range without refuelling: 460 kilometres

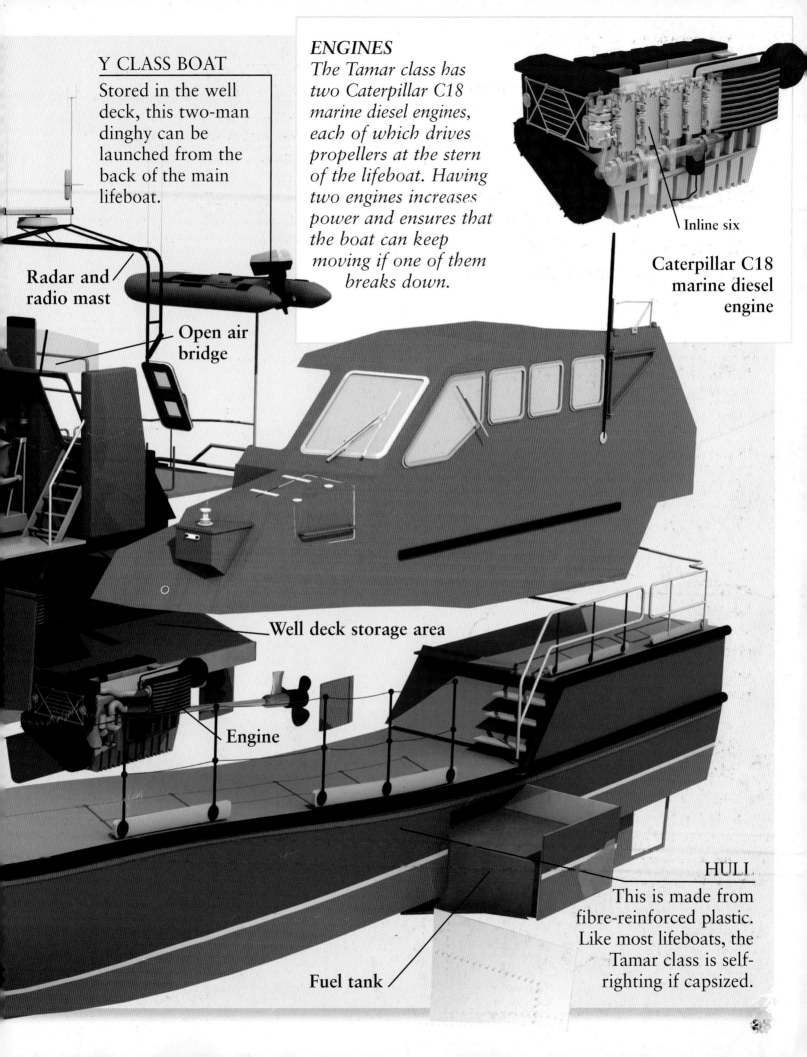

Y CLASS BOAT

Stored in the well deck, this two-man dinghy can be launched from the back of the main lifeboat.

ENGINES

The Tamar class has two Caterpillar C18 marine diesel engines, each of which drives propellers at the stern of the lifeboat. Having two engines increases power and ensures that the boat can keep moving if one of them breaks down.

Inline six

Caterpillar C18 marine diesel engine

Radar and radio mast

Open air bridge

Well deck storage area

Engine

HULL

This is made from fibre-reinforced plastic. Like most lifeboats, the Tamar class is self-righting if capsized.

Fuel tank

FIRE-FIGHTING BOAT

Like any large vehicles, ships are always at risk of catching fire. Many types of boat have been adapted or specially built to act as fire-fighting vessels, putting out fires on ships in ports or out at sea. Most of these fire-fighting boats pump the water they use to douse fires from the ocean around them.

Driveshaft from engine

Water feed

Auxiliary pump

Intake pipes

WATER PUMPS
Water is drawn directly from the sea to be sprayed on to the fire. The pumps are normally driven by diesel engines and pressurise the water so that it shoots from the hoses or cannons with enormous force. The powerful jets of water produced can cross the gaps to burning ships.

NEW YORK CITY FIREBOAT
Length: 39 metres
Width: 9.4 metres
Height: 14.5 metres
Weight: 340 tonnes
Top speed: 14 knots (26 kilometres) per hour

FIRE RESCUE

HULL
Most fire-fighting boats can operate in heavy seas if necessary. Often they have deep hulls, like this one.

CRANE

The water cannons used by fire-fighting boats may be mounted directly on the boats' decks or on top of mobile cranes like this. Cranes have the advantage of height, making it easier to reach burning areas on large ships such as oil tankers.

Water cannon

Operator

RESCUE BOATS

Large fire-fighting boats carry smaller rescue boats, like this one. These smaller boats can be launched to recover people who have fallen or jumped into the water to escape the fire.

Wheel control

FI   RE RESCU   E

ENGINES

Fire-fighting boats vary and so do their engines. One of the largest boats operated by the New York Fire Department is the John D McKean. It is powered by two 1,000 horsepower direct reversible diesel engines. Two more identical engines drive its water pumps.

Cooling systems

Turbocharger

Oil filters

AIR/SEA RESCUE HELICOPTER

Air/sea rescue helicopters may be used together with or instead of lifeboats. They return people to shore more quickly than lifeboats can. Helicopters may also be used to rescue people trapped on cliffs or airlift them from oil rigs, islands or isolated beaches. The Westland Sea King is the main rescue helicopter used around the UK.

Tail rotor

Tail rotor driveshaft

Tailplane

Winch

WESTLAND SEA KING

Rotor diameter: 18.9 metres
Length: 16.7 metres
Height: 5.1 metres
Top speed: 232 kilometres per hour
Range without refuelling: 1,230 kilometres

RESCUE CREW

One crew member operates the winch. Another performs the rescue. The winch operator then helps the rescued person to board the helicopter.

Retractable undercarriage

Hydraulic motor

Cable reel

WINCH

Suspended from the side of the Westland Sea King above the main door, this lowers a rescuer into position while the helicopter hovers above.

Winch hook

EMERGENCY FLOTATION BAGS

Stowed just above the wheels, these can be inflated rapidly if the helicopter has to ditch in the sea.

MAIN BAY

In addition to its four crew members, the Westland Sea King can carry up to six loaded stretchers, or 18 standing and seated survivors.

Radome

ENGINES

The Westland Sea King is powered by two Rolls Royce Gnome engines, positioned just in front of the main rotor blade. A very reliable engine, the Gnome first went into production in 1959.

Rolls Royce Gnome gas turbine

Turbine blades

Exhaust

Intake

MAIN ROTOR

Designed for shipboard operations the five main rotor blades can be folded for easy stowage.

FLIGHT CREW

The Westland Sea King is flown by a pilot and a co-pilot. The largely glass cockpit gives them an excellent field of view, vital for scanning the water below.

Electronics

FUSELAGE

The Sea King has a metal skinned fuselage. The tail section is hinged so that it can be folded.

Fuel tank

HULL

As well as flotation bags, the Sea King has a boat-shaped hull. This is another safety device to prevent it sinking, should it crash-land on water.

AERIAL FIREFIGHTER

Some fires are so large or inaccessible that they can only be dealt with from the air. Known as a 'Super-Scooper' or 'Duck', the Canadair CL-215 is specially designed to fight such blazes. Introduced into service in 1969, the CL-215 scoops water from lakes during a 12-second, 130 kilometre per hour dash over the surface, before returning to the fire with its tanks full.

Fin (Tail)

Elevator

Rudder

Access ladder

CANADAIR CL-215

Wingspan: 28.6 metres
Length: 19.8 metres
Height: 8.9 metres
Top speed: 290 kilometres per hour
Maximum water capacity: 5,299 litres

CONTROL SURFACES

Large ailerons give the Canadair CL-215 increased stability in the air, allowing it to make tight turns.

LANDING FLOATS

Positioned near the wing tips, these stabilise the aircraft when it is floating by preventing the ends of the wings from dipping into the water.

Pratt & Whitney R-2800

Cylinder

Cooling fins

Propshaft

ENGINES
The Canadair CL-215 is powered by two 2,100 hp Pratt and Whitney R-2800 piston engines, mounted on each wing. The R-2800 Double Wasp is a two-row, 18-cylinder, air-cooled radial aircraft engine, first developed in 1938. The Wasp is renowned for its exceptional ruggedness and reliability.

Engine cowling

COCKPIT
This is positioned high up and some distance behind the nose. The cockpit seats the pilot and co-pilot.

WATER TANKS
The Canadair CL-215 can carry up to 5,299 litres of water in its tanks, in the main body of the aircraft. Water reaches the tanks via two tubular probes. These emerge from the hull and are pushed through the water as the plane flies low above the surface. If necessary, foaming agent can be mixed with the water.

Water probe

Overflow

Water tank

Drop door

FUSELAGE
The fuselage of the 'Super-Scooper' is shaped like a boat hull. This enables it to take off from, and land on water. It uses retractable wheels to land on the ground.

FUTURE MACHINES

Many of the rescue services will turn to robotic vehicles in the future. Robots are already used in fire-fighting and rescue operations. They can identify whether certain areas are close to collapse and too dangerous for human teams to enter.

ROSENBAUER PANTHER
Sturdy yet lightweight, the latest airport fire-fighting vehicle is designed for speed and manoeuvrability.

One advance in fire-fighting is the Marsupial Robot – consisting of two robots, one of which supplies electricity while the other investigates dangerous areas with a video camera and transmits pictures back to the supply robot. Ambulances of the future may have cameras fitted inside and outside to help avoid collisions or a device to change red traffic lights to green. A 'shell' concept proposes a removable shell that slides off the ambulance, and creates a temporary treatment place.

VUAV 'EAGLE EYE'
This Vertical Unmanned Aerial Vehicle is designed to be a US Coastguard scout and is launched from the deck of a ship.

CARBON MOTORS E7
Due to enter service in 2012, this US vehicle is the world's first ever purpose-built police car. Among other features, it has built-in lights and sirens, and a cockpit with fully integrated, factory fitted, law enforcement equipment.

GLOSSARY

ailerons
Hinged control sections on the aircraft wing and used to help an aircraft turn.

coxswain
The person who has charge of a lifeboat's crew. The coxswain may also steer the boat if the helmsman becomes unable to.

defibrillator
An electrical device used to counteract heart muscle fibrillation and restore normal heartbeat by applying a brief electric shock. Fibrillation is the uncoordinated twitching of muscle fibres.

diesel
A type of fuel used by motor vehicles. Diesel is normally oil-based but may also be derived from plant material or other organic matter.

dinghy
A small, open-decked boat.

fire hydrant
An upright pipe with a nozzle for drawing water from an underground mains water supply in the event of an emergency.

foaming agent
A substance that is mixed with water to create a thick foam.

GPS
Global Positioning System. A system of satellites that allows people with specialised receivers to pinpoint exactly where they are on the Earth.

helmsman
The person who steers a boat or ship.

hydraulic
Operated by a liquid such as water or oil under high pressure.

internal combustion engine
An engine that burns fuels such as petrol inside cylinders to generate power.

municipal ambulances
Ambulances that are based in towns or cities and used to transport members of the general public.

pike pole
A long-handled instrument used by firefighters to pull away burning debris when tackling a fire.

plexiglass
An extremely tough transparent plastic used as a substitute for glass.

self-righting
Designed to turn itself back upright if tipped over in the water.

ventilator
A device that supplies oxygen or a mixture of oxygen and carbon dioxide for breathing, particularly to a person who is unable to breathe unaided.

INDEX